Balancing the Books and Building Dreams

Shermanetta Carter, CPA

ISBN: 979-8-218-77800-2

New Heights Publishing

Acknowledgements

To the Board of Trustees of Morris Brown College from 2019 until now. Thank you for embracing the vision, standing firm in your governance, and helping us write a new chapter in the legacy of Morris Brown College.

To Dr. Kevin James, nineteenth President of Morris Brown College. This book reflects our shared journey, one marked by resilience, faith, and a steadfast commitment to lifting Morris Brown to new heights. It is an honor to serve alongside you in this #Resurgence of the College's legacy.

To the extraordinary faculty, staff, and students of Morris Brown College who stood firm during the years we carried the weight of being unaccredited. This book is as much yours as it is mine. Thank you for being the keepers of the dream when others counted us out.

To my elementary, junior high, and high school teachers, thank you for being mentors at a time in my life when guidance and encouragement mattered most. You saw promise in me before I could see it in myself, and the lessons you imparted extended far beyond the classroom. For all the moments you invested in molding my mind and spirit, I am deeply grateful.

To my college instructors, thank you for challenging me, inspiring me, and equipping me with the foundation to build a meaningful career. I am especially grateful to Benjamin Strickland, CPA, whose dedication to his craft and his students made all the difference in my journey. **Professor Benjamin Strickland**, CPA, you taught me everything I needed to know about accounting, instilling not just knowledge but a sense of confidence and integrity essential to the profession. Because of your guidance and belief in my potential, I am able to share the story of Morris Brown College—a story shaped by the principles and passion you nurtured within me.

To my beloved Sorority sisters of Alpha Kappa Sorority, Incorporated®, especially my cherished **21 S.O.C.**, my heart overflows with gratitude for the unwavering friendship and sisterhood we have shared. Through every triumph and every trial, you have embraced me with love, lifted me with encouragement, and stood as constant pillars of support. The memories we have created together—the laughter and the tears, the strength found in unity, and the lessons learned in solidarity—have become cornerstones of my life' s journey. Being lifelong friends means sharing not just the celebrations, but also the challenges, and you have never wavered. Thank you for being present through it all, for believing in me, and for reminding me, time and again, of the power and beauty found in true sisterhood. Thank you Squad, Gamma Gamma and Alpha Alpha Pi Omega.

And to Olivia Almagro—my fellow MBC alumnus, book coach, creative ally, and truth-teller—thank you for helping me find my voice and guiding it onto the page with purpose and clarity. This work is a testament to what we build when passion meets partnership.

Dedication

Mom and Dad, you have always placed me in situations beyond my wildest dreams. Your support has opened my eyes to the endless possibilities of pursuing my dreams.

I dedicate this book to my siblings (Alexis, Sye Jr., Shunta, and Terlyn), who have been my lifelong BFFs and cheerleaders, thank you for your unwavering support and for reminding me of the strength that lies within family bonds.

With deepest gratitude to my uncles Leon and Allan Evans and God Mommy Gloria (Asberry) Daniel, I am forever grateful for your financial and emotional support.

This book is a tribute to my nieces and nephews. I hope my journey has inspired you.

With heartfelt thanks to my friends and family. Your encouragement, laughter, and belief in me have fueled my path in ways words cannot fully express.

Foreword

Rev. Dr. Herman "Skip" Mason, Jr. '84

There are few stories in higher education as stirring, as improbable, and as necessary as that of Morris Brown College—a historic beacon of hope, founded by formerly enslaved African Americans in 1881, and revived by faith, fortitude, and fearless leadership more than a century later. This book is not only a chronicle of Morris Brown's triumphant resurgence, but also a testimony to what happens when dreams are not deferred, when legacy is honored, and when resilience becomes strategy.

For over two decades, Morris Brown College stood at a precipice—without accreditation, stripped of federal funding, and left to face what many assumed would be a slow and silent demise. Dr. Kevin James took on what seemed to be an impossible task that he labeled the "Hard Reset." But in 2022, against all odds, accreditation was restored. In that moment, Morris Brown did not just reclaim a status; it reclaimed a future. Its restoration marked more than an administrative victory. It was a cultural and spiritual awakening—an affirmation that Historically Black Colleges and Universities (HBCUs) are not just relevant; they are essential. This rebirth was not singularly done. It stood on the shoulders of those who kept the doors open, alumni and support groups. It was about pulling together the right people for the moment. One of those people was Shermanetta Carter.

Within this broader story of HBCU resilience and Morris Brown's "Lazarus moment" Shermanetta Carter, the college's Chief Financial Officer has written this important book *Balancing the Books and Building Dreams* which offers an intimate view of how revival takes root—not just in grand gestures, but in ledgers balanced, strategies drawn, and decisions made in boardrooms and back offices. At the center of this renaissance stand Ms. Carter, a CPA, and a steward of institutional purpose. Ms. Carter brought to Morris Brown a rare combination of precision and passion, rooted in years of experience and a deep belief in the power of Black education to transform lives. A distinguished graduate of the famed Business and Accounting Department, a member of Alpha Kappa Alpha Sorority and a successful CPA with her own firm, she put her professional and future aspirations on the line for her Alma Mater. It was divinely ordered.

Her leadership was not merely managerial; it was visionary. With strategic planning, fiscal accountability, and a steady hand, she helped navigate a path from chaos to clarity. Her work reminds us that financial stewardship is not only about numbers—it is about narrative. Every spreadsheet she restructured, every audit she faced down, and every plan she implemented carried the weight of generations and the hope of futures yet to be written.

Ms. Carter's journey is deeply personal and profoundly communal. She honors the circle of strength that has sustained her: her clients who trust her expertise, her sorority sisters whose sisterhood uplifts and anchors her, the pastors who pray over her purpose, and the colleagues who walk with her in service and strategy. Together, they represent a constellation of Black excellence and faith-led fortitude that has guided her professionally and spiritually.

As readers, you are invited to experience more than a financial case study. Within these pages, you will discover the art of institutional rebirth—blended with practical tools, hard-won lessons, and stories of courage. You will witness the balancing act of leadership, where faith and numbers meet, where legacy and innovation dance, and where dreams—against all odds—become blueprints for the future.

This book celebrates the sacred work of preserving our institutions and the audacity to dream, build, and rebuild. It asks each of us to consider: What are *we* doing to honor the legacy that shaped us? How are we stewarding the visions entrusted to our care?

In celebrating the restoration of Morris Brown College, Shermanetta Carter affirms a broader truth: we are never too far gone for grace, never too off course to chart a new path. Her work is a call to action—for leaders, dreamers, and builders—to pick up the mantle of transformation and to never stop believing in the power of our collective story.

As the president of Morris Brown's next-door neighbor, the Interdenominational Theological Center who like Morris Brown found itself experiencing so many of the scenarios and financial challenges that she has noted, this book has given me immense hope and direction. There is a path forward and my beloved sister Shermanetta has created a playbook for the ages for HBCU's.

Let this book inspire you to balance your own books, build your own dreams, and honor the institutions that made you.

With admiration and hope,

Rev. Dr. Herman "Skip" Mason, Jr.
Morris Brown College Class of 1984
President, Interdenominational Theological Center

The Call That Changed Everything

Chapter 1

The morning of February 22, 2019, was like any other busy tax season day at my CPA firm, Integrity Accounting Services, LLC. I had no idea that a single phone call would set off a chain of events that would alter the course of my professional life and deepen my commitment to my alma mater, Morris Brown College.

I received a call from my classmate Jeffrey Miller who was at the time, a member of the college's Board of Trustees, and audit committee member, with news that Dr. Kevin James, a native of South Carolina and former CEO of 100 Black Men of Atlanta had been named interim president of Morris Brown. Yet, the urgency in Jeffrey's voice hinted at a deeper problem, one that would soon compel me to make a choice between operating my flourishing CPA firm and the embattled institution I had once called home. Little did I know, I was about to embark on a journey that would challenge my resolve, patience, financial well-being, and commitment to saving my beloved institution from the brink of financial collapse.

I knew Morris Brown would not be able to compensate me or match the six-figure income I was generating through my firm. I was mad when I thought about how I once volunteered my services several years before this meeting, and the previous Administration never followed up. There was no communication, which led me to believe the Board was considering closing my alma mater within the next year because of a lack of oversight by everyone involved.

Jeffrey updated me on the progress Morris Brown had made since losing its accreditation in 2002 and filing for bankruptcy in 2014. However, I was unsure why this news warranted a phone call. Jeffrey insisted that we meet in person to discuss what Dr. James's appointment would mean for MBC's future. I was still wondering why the administration wasn't doing anything to move the college further along and why the CFO wasn't doing his job. Personally, I felt embarrassed that I had not been financially contributing to help. Unfortunately, Black college graduates have a low percentage of donating back to the college after they graduate. According to Forbes, the average rate of alumni giving at the nation's 105 HBCUs is approximately ten percent.

I heard the Board had vetted several CPAs, but I ended up being on the short list to lead the charge. Jeffrey told me he had first called Joaquin Brown, my client and fellow classmate and accounting grad, to find out whether I was qualified to handle the position. Jeffrey mentioned that the Dekalb Alumni Chapter would pay for my services, which they did.

My decision was made after consulting with my family and mentors. One of my mentors and fellow alumni, Dr. Joy Jackson-Guilford, assisted me throughout the decision-making process. She recommended that I compile a list of pros and cons related to assuming this role. If it were logical, she advised me to consider undertaking the task that I felt called to do. She also asked me to pray about it. I followed her guidance, and the outcome is the history I am now documenting.

When he entered my office, Jeffery immediately began sharing information about the financial state of Morris Brown, which was frightening. The school was several months behind on paying its faculty and staff because donations had dried up. At the time Dr. James was named interim president, the chief financial officer was working other jobs and was rarely seen on campus. The accounting books were not being tended to, and the college had not been able to produce audited financial statements dating back to 2014.

Jeffery's list of deficiencies within the fiscal affairs office went on for at least an hour before he admitted that the Board Chairperson warned that he would start proceedings to close the school if we did not achieve re-accreditation under a new administration.

Then, I was totally shocked when he asked me if I was interested in taking on the role as CFO under the new administration. I said, "No, but good luck!" By that time, it had taken me ten years to grow my CPA firm with nonprofits, faith-based organizations, and affluent clients. They trusted me, and through their referrals, my firm was thriving.

However, my conversation with Jeffrey didn't end with my rejection of his invitation. He continued to emphasize the need for "clean" financial statements to present to our stakeholders, auditors, and the Transnational Association of Christian Colleges and Schools (TRACS) accrediting agency. His persistence, combined with my commitment to Morris Brown, led me to reconsider. I agreed that my firm would be open to entering into a formal contract to assist the interim CFO with preparing the financial statements.

The Southern Association of Colleges and Schools (SACS) revoked Morris Brown College's accreditation in 2002 after it was discovered that the college's president, Dr. Delores Cross, and financial aid director, Dr. Parvesh Singh, had misappropriated federal funds. The college knowingly falsified enrollment data to increase the number of students receiving financial aid, some of whom never attended, and then used the millions of dollars fraudulently obtained to cover operational costs. Some students were registered but had never attended the college. This led to an investigation by the Department of Education. As a result, Morris Brown was obligated to pay back over five million dollars. The matter was settled during the bankruptcy. This loss of accreditation led to a financial crisis that nearly forced the college to close.

The administration signed the agreement with my CPA firm in May of 2019. Upon walking into the CFO's office, the first day of my assignment, I felt angry. There were piles of paper so high on the interim CFO's desk that I couldn't see the top of it, and boxes of important documents lay all over the floor.

When I started digging through, I even found envelopes that had not been opened, which contained checks as donations. I looked outside the windows and saw that Fountain Hall, which is a registered National Historic Landmark and the oldest surviving building of the Atlanta University Center, and Griffin Hightower (GH), the building where W.E.B. Du Bois wrote his book, *The Souls of Black Folks*, had broken windows. During my matriculation from 1989 until 1994, GH was a multi-purpose building used as classrooms, laboratories, a lecture hall, offices, and a library. I later learned that homeless people were sleeping inside the buildings. I also noticed the vacancy across the street, an empty plot that used to be my old dormitory, Sarah Allen Quadrangle. Sarah Allen was the wife of Richard Allen, the founder of the African Methodist Episcopal Church (AMEC).

For the first time, I cried and wondered if I had taken on more than I was capable of handling. Yes, I received my accounting degree in 1994, then went on to work for the IRS, the public accounting sector, and eventually started my CPA firm, but I was at a loss as to where to start at Morris Brown and had no staff to help me figure out what to do next.

Within two months of starting the project, the interim CFO resigned because she preferred her career in the financial services industry. Again, Jeffery recommended me to Bishop Jackson and Dr. James. For at least one year, there was no permanent CFO at the helm of the fiscal affairs office. On top of that, there were alumni and friends who were upset and did not believe we could ever regain accreditation. They did not believe in this administration. However, they continued to donate.

My firm was still under contract to prepare financial statements for reporting, and I pitched in when I could to at least process payroll to get caught up on paying faculty and staff. We were behind on payroll by at least seven pay periods. By this time, my firm wasn't getting paid, and I was ecstatic when we finally became and remained current around mid-August.

In May 2020, we scored another major win by paying off our Georgia Power bill, which at one point had an outstanding balance as high as $72,000. We were able to do that because we set up a separate portal with Georgia Power for donors to pay directly to them rather than Morris Brown to ensure that the payments went directly to the vendor. We were in the middle of the COVID-19 pandemic and qualified for and received the Paycheck Protection Program (PPP) loan. We used $20,000 of $90,975 received from the Small Business Administration through Citizens Trust Bank to apply to the balance.

In the meantime, my CPA firm was declining because I was not in my office, taking care of my clients and managing my staff. I was scared that I would lose the financial footing I worked so hard to grow. My dream was to have a huge, regional firm. However, at this rate, I didn't see myself moving toward that career goal. The work in righting the ship at MBC was taking over, and I began to ponder my next steps. Should I walk away from my CPA firm or from MBC?

By this time, however, the fight to restore Morris Brown College wasn't just professional; it had become personal. The weight of its legacy, the stories of alumni who had walked those halls with pride, and the hope of future generations counting on the institution's survival—all of it stirred something deep within me. I wasn't just battling numbers on a balance sheet anymore; I was standing in defense of a dream deferred.

Staying on the course became a matter of principle. There were long nights, countless meetings, and moments when the weight of what had to be done felt almost unbearable. But giving up was never an option.

My job went beyond cleaning up the books. I was determined to build a system—a strong, transparent, and accountable financial foundation—that would outlive my time and serve as a shield against the kind of collapse Morris Brown had endured. I wanted to ensure that this situation would never, ever be repeated. Not on my watch. And not on anyone else's after me.

In July of 2020, I was officially appointed as the permanent full-time CFO at Morris Brown. Dr. James announced it on his Facebook page, so I felt even more compelled to see the re-accreditation through to the end. However, I was also struggling with the dilemma of walking away to rebuild my firm, which was my pride and joy.

I didn't want to let my fellow alumni down, so I continued to press through. I even called a classmate to ask him to take over as CFO. His response of "No way!" didn't shock me. So, I kept moving on with this God-ordained journey, not knowing that even my accounting degree from Morris Brown, CPA license, and professional skills could prepare me for this venture.

All the steps toward advancing my career prepared me to rescue my alma mater from a downfall that most believed we could never recover from. There was also excitement from alumni, City of Atlanta and State officials, the AME Church, and other HBCUs and colleges who were watching us in hopes of helping them to become re-accredited across the country and to see us make history. No other college had lost its accreditation and then regained it twenty-plus years later.

I took on a lot of pressure to make it happen, knowing that it had to start with financial stability. Still, by this time, I felt I could not back out. The support from alumni, colleagues, and my sister, Alexis, who was the first of us to attend an integrated school when she was in third grade, as well as my home town crew was so overwhelming that I also began to believe that we were on the verge of making history with the biggest comeback of all time.

Chapter 2

The fourth of five children, I was born and raised in Montgomery, Alabama, the birthplace of the civil rights movement. It was the site of the historic 1955 bus boycott, led by Rosa Parks, who refused to give up her seat to a white passenger. Montgomery is also known for "Bloody Sunday," which took place on March 7, 1965, in Selma, Alabama, when peaceful marchers were brutally attacked by police as they walked from Selma to Montgomery. The marchers included Hosea Williams (class of 1951), Martin Luther King, Jr., Ralph Abernathy, Jessie Jackson, John Lewis (The Boy from Troy, Alabama), and Joseph Lowery among others. My mom and dad, Linda (Evans) and Sye Carter, were both graduates of Booker T. Washington High School.

Although Brown vs. Board of Education was passed in 1954, which mandated that states desegregate schools, the public schools were still segregated by the time my oldest sister Alexis started elementary school until 1975, when she entered the third grade at Bear Elementary School. The rest of us, Sye Jr., Shunta, I and Terlyn, followed her from elementary school to Cloverdale Junior High and Jefferson Davis High Schools. Cloverdale was later purchased by Huntington College, and Jefferson Davis was later renamed to Johnson Abernathy Graetz (JAG) High School.

My dad worked in a glass factory until it closed during my elementary school years, after which he attended Trenholm Tech, a local historically black community college, to become an auto body mechanic. We always had food, nice clothes, and enjoyed summers at the YMCA, where I learned to swim. Those were good times, though I didn't fully appreciate them back then.

My maternal grandmother passed away before I was born, and I remember my mom's younger brothers living with us until they finished high school. Both joined the military—one in the Navy and the other in the Marine Corps. We loved watching wrestling on TV, and I vividly recall a time when my uncles were practicing moves and accidentally broke Alexis's leg. She was rushed to the hospital, and of course, my uncles got a whooping. Even though my mom was their sister, she had to act as their mother too. Those were more good times.

During my time in public school, I had the privilege of being taught by exceptional Black educators who also served as mentors. I have particularly fond memories of Ms. Tarrant, my fifth-grade teacher. She graduated from Alabama State University in the late 1960s and embarked on a career as an elementary school teacher. Ms. Tarrant not only delivered academic instruction but also motivated us to pursue our life goals and contribute to our communities. She once remarked to me when I was older, "I didn't have to teach you. You knew what you had to do." Her insight proved accurate, as many Black students from my high school class pursued careers as politicians, engineers, lawyers, doctors, professional athletes, executives, and entrepreneurs. Even more than forty years later, we remain in contact, and her telephone number is saved in my phone.

I had other friends during my junior and high school years who came from a legacy of history makers. Janay Smith was one of them. Her father was the late Jock Smith, who was a senior partner with Johnny Cochran at their firm in Tuskegee, Alabama. Her mother, Yvette Smiley-Smith, was one of the first black CPAs in the state of Alabama. She was successful in her CPA firm as a forensic and expert witness in legal proceedings across the country. Janay went on to graduate from Howard University, Samford University and Stanford University. Notably, she was an attorney for The Cochran Firm with her father. Currently, she is a care advocate speaker, podcast host, caregiver and comedian.

When I reached high school, race relations in Montgomery remained a struggle. Black and white students had separate homecoming attendants, and being part of a segregated homecoming court had a profound impact on our school community.

In my senior year, 1989, I was the Black Homecoming attendant, and my best friend, Dionne Jordan, became the second Black Homecoming queen in the school's history. Her father is Reverend Thomas Jordan, Sr. At the young age of twenty-three, he became the pastor of Lilly Baptist Church. That was almost sixty years ago, and he baptized Reverend Martin Luther King, Jr. in 1956. While many of us were too young to fully grasp the implications, it sparked important conversations about identity, representation, and inclusiveness. Though most students formed friendships across racial lines, the homecoming rules were out of our control. In the end, it served as a catalyst for ongoing dialogue, reminding us that the journey toward true inclusivity was far from over.

It came as no surprise to my friends and family when I chose Morris Brown College, a private AME institution founded by former slaves and steeped in history. My older sister Alexis attended Morris Brown, and my other sisters and I followed her. The contrast between my high school and Morris Brown was like night and day. Yet, I felt ready and prepared to embrace this new chapter.

****

Attending Morris Brown College was more than just a personal milestone for me; it was a continuation of a legacy that had been deeply rooted in my family for generations.

It began with my fourth cousin on my mother's side, Rosalind Range, who first blazed the trail. Rosalind enrolled in Morris Brown in 1970, and by 1974, she had earned her Bachelor of Science in Secretarial Science. While at the college, she became a proud member of the Gamma Zeta Chapter of Delta Sigma Theta Sorority, Incorporated. That was in the fall of 1971. She wasn't just a scholar; she was also a homecoming attendant, Miss Delta, Miss Omega, and a cheerleader.

Rosalind fondly recalls an era when Morris Brown's band, football, and basketball teams were the best around. One vivid memory she shared was the night of the Muhammad Ali fight in Atlanta during her freshman year. She sat on the porch of Sarah Allen Quadrangle (SAQ), watching as luxury cars rolled down the street toward the Paschal Hotel on MLK. The women wore fur coats, and the men were impeccably dressed. It was a magical time. Rosalind went on to become a flight attendant for Delta International, serving for eighteen years before retiring from Omni Air in 2012.

The next chapter of our family's legacy at Morris Brown began with my sister Alexis, who enrolled in 1985. She was the first of the four sisters to graduate from college, earning her degree in Criminal Justice in 1989. Alexis also made history in our family by becoming the first of us to join the Gamma Gamma Chapter of Alpha Kappa Alpha Sorority, Incorporated®. It was her initiation that earned us the nickname of #CarterGirls.

After graduation, Alexis became a Deputy Sheriff in our hometown, and was later promoted to investigator. She continued the tradition of excellence, becoming a middle school English Language Arts teacher. She is certified in Gifted Education, Reading Specialist, and Administration, and holds both a master's degree in Curriculum Instruction and a Specialist degree in Educational Leadership. Today, she teaches at a military base in Kentucky under the Department of Defense Education Activity (DODEA).

My sister, Shunta Carter-Lacey, followed Alexis to Morris Brown in 1989. Shunta, ever the athlete, became a cheerleader and was actively involved in student government (SGA). She earned her Bachelor of Science in Management, Entrepreneurship, and Technology. Like Alexis, Shunta also pursued a career in education and now teaches middle school ELA for DODEA. Over the years, she's taught at Fort Moore in Georgia, Stuttgart in Germany, and currently teaches at an elementary/middle school in Laurel Bay, South Carolina. She, too, holds a certification in Science and a Master's in Curriculum Instruction, along with a Specialist degree in Educational Leadership.

As for me, I embarked on my Morris Brown journey in the fall of 1989. By 1994, I had earned my Bachelor of Science in Accounting. My college years were filled with opportunities— I was part of the Marching Wolverine Band, Mock Trial team, competed in track and field, and served in the SGA. I was also honored to be the sophomore homecoming attendant. During my time on the Mock Trial team, we traveled to Des Moines, Iowa, to participate in a nationwide competition. The only states I had visited prior to this experience were Six Flags in Georgia and Panama City Beach in Florida.

The path to success wasn't without its challenges. Financial aid played a crucial role in our ability to attend college. Our parents were always supportive, but with limited financial resources, they couldn't save for our education. Alexis discovered the Federal Pell Grant, and it became a lifeline for us. We qualified based on financial need, and Shunta and I also benefited from a sibling waiver since we attended Morris Brown simultaneously. With the Pell grants, sibling waiver, and the diligent work of our student accounts advisors, we were able to achieve our dreams.

One summer, my excitement for life in Atlanta and at Morris Brown was so strong that I chose not to go home. Dorms were closed, so I had to figure out how to afford off-campus living. One night, as my suitemate Tenga and I sat in our Resident Assistant's room—since we couldn't afford our own TV—an Army commercial for the Buddy Team Enlistment Option came on. We both talked about it, but in the end, only I enlisted. It turned out to be one of the best decisions I made.

After enlisting, I joined the track and field team to prepare for basic training, running the four-by-one hundred relay. After being assigned to my Army Reserve Unit, one of my Army buddies, Eudora, became one of my best friends, and we've remained close friends for over thirty years.

I spent eleven years in the Army Reserves as a photojournalist and was honorably discharged after achieving the rank of sergeant. A memorable moment during my enlistment was when I traveled with a Command Sergeant Major of the Army in a helicopter to various Georgia military bases to meet soldiers and tell the Army's story through their eyes. All of my student loans were paid off as a result of the GI Bill. I no longer had any debt to Morris Brown College or to the Department of Education.

During my sophomore year, I was one of only three accounting students accepted for an internship with the IRS. Despite being younger than many of the other candidates, I was selected over juniors and seniors with more experience. We were flown to Milwaukee, Wisconsin, for six weeks of training, my first time flying so far from home. Our manager became like a big brother, and I even invited him to judge the Mr. Ebony Man pageant on behalf of my sorority. Although I no longer work at the IRS, he remains a close friend.

My fellow MBC interns and I also shared a unique experience that forged lifelong friendships. Marcus, one of my peers, still works at the IRS and now holds a management position, while Chenita transitioned into education and teaches math in Atlanta Public Schools.

A defining moment in my Morris Brown journey came in the spring of 1991, when my sister Shunta and I both joined the Gamma Gamma Chapter of Alpha Kappa Alpha Sorority, Incorporated®. Although Rosalind had joined Delta Sigma Theta, we followed in the footsteps of my oldest sister. We were inspired by the women of Alpha Kappa Alpha. They were leaders in our community—graceful, intelligent, and dedicated to service. After attending several AKA events, I knew I had found my home. The warmth, sisterhood, and support I experienced from the members cemented my decision. I was even a bridesmaid in several of my Sorority sisters' weddings after we graduated.

As an AKA, my three sisters and I are proud to carry on the legacy of service, scholarship, and sisterhood that has spanned over a century. Today, two of my nieces are also members of this illustrious sorority.

The final #CarterGirl to attend Morris Brown was my younger sister Terlyn, the last of the #Carter5, who enrolled in 1994. Like her sisters before her, Terlyn was a cheerleader. She graduated in 1998 with a Bachelor of Science in Therapeutic Recreation and has since transitioned into elementary education, teaching in various schools in Montgomery, Alabama.

Our second cousin, Taron Williams, entered college in 1999 and graduated with a Bachelor of Science in Sociology, focusing on Family Counseling. He pledged Zeta Chapter of Phi Beta Sigma in the Spring of 2002 and was heavily involved in campus life. Taron directed the choir, served as a Resident Assistant, and led the gospel choir on tours. Today, he holds an MSW and MSEd in Higher Education Administration and is completing a Principal Preparation Program at the University of Delaware. He works as a Restorative Practice Coordinator at KUUMBA Academy Charter School in Wilmington, Delaware.

In 2024, I was deeply honored to receive the Tyrone Fletcher Award at the Tower of Strength Homecoming Gala. This award recognizes families with multiple generations of graduates, numerous siblings or relatives, and outstanding contributions to Morris Brown College. I am humbled that my family is part of this rich and enduring legacy.

Chapter 3

I had always dreamed of launching my own accounting firm, driven by a deep desire to serve small businesses, faith-based nonprofits, and churches that needed guidance. The odds were stacked against me—starting a business in the middle of a recession wasn't exactly a conventional path to success. But I knew my faith was stronger than any challenge the economy could throw at me. No matter the obstacles, nothing could stop me from pursuing my dream.

When I graduated from Morris Brown in 1994, my focus was on building my career, even though I hadn't yet earned my Certified Public Accountant (CPA) license. As time passed, I realized that to continue climbing the corporate ladder, I needed that certification. After sitting for the exam seven times, I finally achieved my goal in 2006. I was proud to join the elite two percent of Black CPAs and, even more so, the mere one percent of Black women in the industry.

The odds were discouraging, but I didn't let them define me. I resolved to press forward with blinders on, ignoring the distractions around me. After earning my CPA license, I felt a shift. The corporate world no longer held the same allure it once did. I found myself reminiscing about the freedom my father had when he owned his auto body shop—working hard for months and then taking time to relax, reaping the benefits of his labor. It sparked something in me, and I knew then that I wanted to become an entrepreneur.

By 2007, I had explored a variety of roles in government, public, and corporate accounting. I even served as CFO of a small nonprofit for a time, but none of it brought the fulfillment I was searching for. I realized that my true passion was helping small businesses and nonprofits succeed.

The Great Recession was looming, triggered by the housing market collapse. It was a time of uncertainty and financial upheaval, but where others saw fear, I saw opportunity.

In November 2007, I took a leap of faith. I left my full-time CFO job, walked away from a part-time gig at a well-established accounting firm, and decided it was time to carve out my own niche. The risks were high, but the need for sound accounting advice was greater. By January 2008, I had registered Integrity Accounting Services, LLC, rented a modest office space—just enough for a desk, a computer, and a couple of chairs—and prepared for tax season. My business plan was only half-finished, and I had no marketing experience, but I relied on my network. I plugged all my contacts—family, friends, and my sorority sisters—into Constant Contact. And it worked!

By April 15, 2008, I had processed seventy-five tax returns. It was a promising start, but it wasn't enough to sustain me. Like many Americans at the time, I faced the possibility of losing my home. Business was slow, and I hadn't yet mastered marketing. I remember borrowing gas money from one of my mentors, Yul Crawford, just to meet with potential clients. It was humbling, but I kept pushing, knowing that hard work would eventually yield results.

My first clients were small businesses, hesitant to trust a new firm in such uncertain times. They couldn't pay me in full, but I accepted what they could offer, grateful for the opportunity to serve. Slowly but surely, my expertise and genuine care for their success began to win them over. I worked long hours, often burning the midnight oil, to ensure they received the best service possible. And as word of mouth spread, more businesses came seeking my help.

As my firm grew, I hired Kendra, a like-minded woman from my church who shared my vision and work ethic. Together, we weathered the recession, helping our clients not only survive but thrive. Integrity Accounting Services became known for its reliability, its commitment to integrity, and its personalized service. By the time the economy began to recover, my firm was well-established, proving that with faith, hard work, and perseverance, success could be built even in the most challenging times.

By 2010, I was able to pay myself a consistent salary. But just when it seemed like things were finally falling into place, life threw another curveball. That year, I was diagnosed with breast cancer. It started at a health fair at my church, where I mentioned to a nurse that my nipple had started inverting. She urged me to get a mammogram. From that appointment came more tests—an ultrasound, an MRI—and finally, the diagnosis.

The words "You have breast cancer" echoed in my mind. I couldn't process anything else. Shunta, my sister, was with me, taking notes and informing the rest of the family about the treatment plan. I remember asking God, "Why me, and why now?" His response was clear: "Because I have work for you to do."

It took months before I scheduled an appointment with the oncologist. I was focused on finishing client projects to build a financial cushion, believing I'd only need chemotherapy and radiation. It sounds reckless, but God honored my faith.

I held tight to Psalm 34:1: "I will bless the Lord at all times; His praise shall continually be in my mouth." Slowly, I began to understand that the work God had for me was bigger than accounting. It was about sharing my testimony, even in the darkest moments.

Throughout everything, my clients stayed loyal. Dr. Sherry Gaither, a valued client, a pastor, and a renowned speaker and author, prayed for me upon learning of my diagnosis. She continued as my client until I closed my business, and she still mentors me today. In the beginning, I had no idea that she was an acquaintance of Dr. Antoinette Alvarado, another pastor with the same credentials. They both ended up being my clients and life coaches. Others sent prayers, support, and love. And God, in His grace, carried me through. After chemotherapy, radiation, a mastectomy and reconstruction of my right breast, I was declared cancer-free in 2012.

By 2013, my firm was growing faster than ever. I moved the office to Chamblee, Georgia, anticipating expansion. I hired new staff, including interns and a full-time accountant, and welcomed my niece, Kayla, during her summers from Savannah State University. But the challenges weren't over. When Snowmageddon hit Atlanta in 2014, my entire team was stranded on the roads for hours, while one of my colleagues, Lakia, had to camp out in the office for five days. Despite the chaos, we remained grateful, and our bond as a team only grew stronger.

As time passed, the firm continued to evolve. Kendra eventually spread her wings, moving on to new opportunities. Though bittersweet, it was a proud moment, knowing I had mentored her to success. My firm relocated to Atlanta, attracting a diverse clientele—from Jewish community centers to real estate associations—and my reputation as one of the one percent of Black female CPAs with my own firm grew. Little did I know that my next calling would take me back to where it all began: dear ole Morris Brown College.

Chapter 4

Driving toward campus felt surreal. Over thirty years ago, I walked these grounds as a student, brimming with hope and ambition. Now, I was returning, not as a student, but as part of a small, dedicated team tasked with breathing new life into this one hundred forty four-year- old institution. The weight of that responsibility hit me the moment I stepped into my office. Stacks of papers covered the desk, and boxes overflowing with files were scattered across the room. I stood there, taking it all in, and thought: *What have I gotten myself into?*

Officially, my first full-time day as CFO was July 1, 2020. Before that, I began in May 2019 as a part-time contractor through my firm. At the time, Morris Brown was still struggling to pay staff consistently, so I chose to adopt a hybrid schedule.

My first day in the role was anything but smooth. I met with the outgoing CFO to get a sense of what she had been tasked with. Like me, she was self-employed and had been balancing her duties with running her financial services firm. Instead of providing actionable solutions, she mainly outlined the problems she had faced. After she resigned to focus on her business, I inherited the chaos, including at least ninety voicemail messages I had to sift through just to begin untangling the issues at hand.

She had been there for at least two months before I came onboard. The CFO before her had rarely set foot on campus. Like the rest of the staff, he wasn't receiving a regular paycheck and had taken on other accounting jobs around Metro Atlanta to support his family.

We were months behind on paying property insurance and struggling to cover basic operational expenses, like Georgia Power and City of Atlanta Water. Although civil rights activist C.T. Vivian championed a campaign in 2008 to raise funds when the school's water was turned off, we were still unable to maintain the expenses after our account was paid in full. Payroll was at least five pay periods overdue. I stood there, overwhelmed, wondering: *Where am I supposed to start?*

The thought of walking away crossed my mind more than once. I was still debating whether I should return to focusing a hundred percent on growing my CPA firm. However, I was angry—angry at the dire condition my alma mater was in and at how far things had fallen, and that anger pushed me forward.

The buildings where I once took classes were now abandoned and unfit for use. The dorms I remembered so vividly had been demolished. The football stadium, where I played in the band and ran track, was sold during the 2015 bankruptcy process.

Did I cry? Absolutely.

The thought of leading a team to restore any resemblance of the lively, thriving institution I attended from 1989 to 1994 felt impossible. When I left the campus that day, I was convinced I wouldn't fulfill the contractual obligation I had committed to. It seemed like it was too late for redemption.

But my family, friends, and fellow alumni kept encouraging me. They believed in me, even when I doubted myself. Slowly, I began to believe that maybe, just maybe, I could make a difference. So, I kept showing up, determined to try and bring hope back to the place that had once given so much to me.

The previous CFO agreed to meet with me one Saturday to discuss what needed to be done with the accounting records to move forward. Together, we prioritized the critical task of ensuring that all financial transactions from the past six years were accurately entered into the accounting system. We also needed to account for any outstanding bills so we could identify exactly who we owed and how much.

That meant meticulously reviewing every document on the desk to determine what was relevant to the task at hand. The project took nearly a month to complete since there was no additional accounting staff to assist me. Searching for outstanding bills felt like looking for a needle in a haystack.

I gained access to the previous president and CFO's emails, combing through them for anything accounting-related that could impact the financial statements. Thankfully, the Assistant Vice President of Institutional Advancement, Todd Blackburn, kept excellent records. Because of his diligence, we were able to properly account for all donations from alumni and other stakeholders.

In addition to sorting through the finances, I was also responsible for managing students' tuition and payment plans. At the time, we had approximately twenty-eight students enrolled for that academic period.

We were making slow but steady progress, so you can imagine my shock when, on June 1, 2019, I received a call from Jerome Rowland, the Director of Operations, informing me that the president's office had caught fire. To make matters worse, the insurance had lapsed, leaving us scrambling to figure out our next steps.

In the end, we had to raise the funds ourselves to restore the building. The fire had triggered the sprinklers, and water seeped through the walls, damaging the first floor as well. It was yet another hurdle in our uphill battle to rebuild the institution.

Remediation efforts included replacing the carpet throughout the building, opening up walls to dry them out, and rebuilding damaged areas. The entire building was filled with smoke, so we kept all the doors open and used fans to clear it out. The cleanup process took more than five months.

During that time, we alternated between working from home and coming into the building a few days a week, determined to maintain steady progress on the reaccreditation process despite the challenges.

It became apparent that Morris Brown wasn't alone in its financial struggles. Many other HBCUs across the country were facing similar challenges. These institutions are often underfunded due to systemic inequities, declining state and federal support, and difficulties in building large endowments. These financial obstacles have severely limited their ability to invest in updated facilities and expand scholarship opportunities for their students.

Despite losing federal government support, Morris Brown College had to devise innovative strategies to sustain itself. The institution relied on alumni donations, formed strategic corporate partnerships, and launched aggressive fundraising campaigns. Filing for bankruptcy helped eliminate a significant portion of its debt, but it came at a steep cost: key campus buildings, including the John H. Lewis Gymnasium, the Towers, and the Sarah Allen dormitory, were sold, with some later demolished.

While many assume that significant changes began during the reaccreditation process, the truth is that alumni and the AME Church remained steadfast in their commitment to the college. Efforts were already in motion well before accreditation was restored. These early initiatives laid the groundwork and made the reaccreditation process more seamless, underscoring the resilience and determination of the Morris Brown community to rebuild and thrive.

Despite facing immense challenges, Morris Brown College never stopped moving forward. Though it operated on a much smaller scale—at one point with fewer than twenty students, all on scholarships funded by private donors—it remained steadfast in its mission to produce Black professionals in medicine, law, STEM, and beyond. But this perseverance came at a cost. Tenured professors were not paid. In fact, most staff members went years without seeing a paycheck. They were later paid retroactively.

Among these unsung heroes was Dr. Nasrolah Farokhi, a professor at Morris Brown since 1981, whose commitment to the college went far beyond the classroom. In one extraordinary act of sacrifice, he mortgaged his own home to help cover the school's utility bills and payroll during a time of dire need.

Dr. Farokhi's journey to Morris Brown began far from Atlanta. Born in Iran, he earned a degree in Social Science and Literature from Tehran University before moving to the United States in the late 1960s to pursue his Master's in Business Administration at Ball State University. In 1981, he joined Morris Brown as an assistant professor, teaching American government and public administration. Over the years, he became a cornerstone of the college community.

Farokhi didn't just teach; he served. He was the Faculty Representative to the Board of Trustees, Special Assistant to the President under two administrations, and managed non-academic support services ranging from facilities management to campus security and even the post office. His tireless dedication and resourcefulness were instrumental in keeping the college afloat during its most precarious times.

When he retired in 2024, the Morris Brown Board of Trustees honored his legacy by renaming the school's Center for Teaching, Learning, and Innovation as The Nasrolah Farokhi Center for Teaching, Learning, and

Innovation. He was also named Professor Emeritus, a title befitting his decades of service and sacrifice.

Dr. Farokhi's story is a testament to the resilience and selflessness that define the Morris Brown community. His unwavering commitment to the college and its mission serves as an enduring reminder of what is possible when we give not just our skills, but our very hearts, to a cause we believe in. The college's long-term stability hinges on consistent investments, modernized infrastructure, and increased public support to ensure its success for generations to come.

Chapter 5

When the Board of Trustees announced Dr. James as interim president in 2019, it felt like a shift was finally happening—a moment where hope started to outweigh despair. His leadership brought a renewed sense of purpose to Morris Brown College, sparking donations from individuals, foundations, and corporations who believed in his bold vision for our beloved institution. It was as if, for the first time in years, we could see a glimmer of light at the end of a very long tunnel.

The AME Church played a critical role during this time, providing not only financial support but also the kind of steadfast encouragement that kept us going when the road felt impossibly steep. Yet, even with their backing, there were moments when the weight of the challenge threatened to crush us. Doubts crept in more than once, whispering that perhaps we were chasing an impossible dream.

But the real heartbeat of Morris Brown College has always been its alumni and supporters. They were the steady force that carried us through our darkest days. When reaccreditation seemed like a distant fantasy and the threat of closure loomed over us like a storm cloud, they stood firm. We gave what we could—our money, our time, our talents—all driven by a shared love for the school that had given us so much.

The National Alumni Association, local chapters, and affinity groups were relentless. They didn't just talk about saving Morris Brown—they acted. They organized fundraisers, recruited students, and poured their energy into keeping the college alive. When our Administration building needed a new roof, they pooled resources and paid for it themselves. They tackled critical repairs and made sure we could continue operating, no matter how dire things seemed.

And everywhere they went, they proudly represented us. They wore their school colors, sported Morris Brown paraphernalia, and reminded the world—and us—that the spirit of Morris Brown had never dimmed. Our doors had never truly closed, and as long as we had each other, they never would.

An alumna from the Class of 1953 quietly became a lifeline for over two hundred students, helping them secure the financial aid they needed to pursue their education. Her commitment to Morris Brown didn't stop there. When she passed away in 2019, she left a remarkable gift of nearly one million dollars to the college, a donation that stands as one of the largest in our history.

Her generosity made a tangible difference, helping to repay debt, meet payroll, and fund critical repairs. It also allowed the college to demonstrate positive cash flow to stakeholders and TRACS, signaling a brighter future for Morris Brown.

To honor her extraordinary legacy, the Board of Trustees approved renaming our executive boardroom in her memory, a permanent tribute to her love for Morris Brown and her belief in its mission.

After we laid out a budget for the reaccreditation process, it became clear that raising funds specifically for this purpose would be crucial. Reaccreditation wasn't just a milestone; it was a lifeline. We needed every dollar accounted for, and so, we reached out to an alumnus from the Class of 1980.

He was no ordinary graduate. As a CPA and the first African American auto dealer group owner to achieve one billion in annual sales, he had built a career defined by trailblazing success. When we shared our plans, he didn't hesitate. He donated one hundred percent of the funds we needed. His generosity covered everything, including audit fees, TRACS application fees, and even the temporary accounting services needed to support my office during this critical time.

It was a gift that didn't just meet a need; it gave us hope. A couple of years later, this extraordinary alumnus joined the Board of Trustees, continuing to shape the future of Morris Brown College in meaningful ways.

By July 2020, we were staring down what seemed like an impossible task: transforming our financial statements to reflect a journey from bankruptcy and debt to a financially stable institution of higher learning. How could we even begin?

I turned to prayer first, as I often do, and then to people. I reached out to colleagues and my former accounting instructor, seeking guidance and clarity on how to execute such a monumental task. Their advice and encouragement were invaluable, but we still needed more support.

Together, we rolled up our sleeves, determined to rewrite the financial narrative of Morris Brown. What had once seemed insurmountable began to feel achievable, piece by piece, as we moved closer to the dream of reaccreditation.

Establishing the accounting systems required for TRACS compliance was anything but straightforward. Reconciling years of unresolved debts often meant sitting across the table from creditors, hammering out settlement agreements, and, at times, reliving old battles. These negotiations frequently led me to Dr. Pritchett, whose sharp memory and firsthand knowledge of the events that had brought us to this point were invaluable. Each conversation was a reminder of how much history—and resilience—were woven into the fabric of Morris Brown College.

But whenever the doubts began to consume me, I drew strength from the spirit of the Morris Brown community. Our alumni and supporters refused to let the story of this institution end here. Even when reaccreditation felt like a distant hope and the shadow of permanent closure loomed large, they showed up.

Their dedication was a lifeline, a steady reminder that we were not alone in this fight. It wasn't just about compliance or financial statements; it was about preserving a legacy built on faith, determination, and a belief in the power of education to transform lives. That belief carried me through, even on the hardest days, as we inched closer to the dream of reaccreditation.

Once I determined that MBC had enough operating and reserve cash, we could finally shift our focus to transforming our financial story from bankruptcy and unpaid debt to one of sustainability and even excess cash flow. But having a goal and having a plan are two different things. What was the plan?

I leaned heavily on my twelve years of experience running my own CPA firm. Those years had taught me how to tackle complex problems head-on, but this task was monumental. I consulted colleagues, tapped into the wisdom of my former accounting instructor, and slowly pieced together a plan of execution.

What came next was nothing short of painstaking. We combed through every unopened envelope left on the former CFO's desk, sifted through boxes scattered across the floor, and scoured storage areas for records dating back to 2016 and beyond. Our primary goal was to close the timeline gap left open by our last audit in 2015. It wasn't just a matter of organizing papers; it was about reconstructing history, piece by piece.

I can't overstate the value of Todd Blackburn, Class of 1990 and a pillar of Morris Brown College. With over thirty years of service as Assistant Vice President for Institutional Advancement and Director of Alumni Affairs, Todd brought unmatched knowledge to the table. Together, we worked to unravel donation records and categorize the incredible generosity of our donors. Each gift told a story, and we had to make sure those stories were clear and compelling.

The accounting team dug deep into the financial records to identify who we owed and who owed us. It became a race against time to reach out to debtors, negotiate settlements, and tie up loose ends. Every phone call, every meeting, every agreement was another step toward a brighter financial future.

The goal was simple yet monumental: to demonstrate that Morris Brown College's bills were current, its old debts resolved, and its financial foundation rebuilt. It wasn't just about numbers on a page; it was about showing the world and ourselves that Morris Brown could rise again.

Under the leadership of Dr. James and Laurie M. Thomas, Esquire, Morris Brown College faced one of its most daunting challenges: addressing a $3.5 million debt owed to the AME Church. This debt, a holdover from our 2015 bankruptcy, loomed over us like a storm cloud. We were in default, with no payments made—a glaring obstacle to proving financial stability to TRACS.

In 2019, we sat down with an AME Church committee to present our case. The stakes couldn't have been higher. Eliminating this debt was not just important; it was essential. Without it, reaccreditation would remain out of reach. As we laid out our situation, we also proposed a bold solution: a $1.5 million scholarship program for AME Church students in exchange for debt forgiveness.

It wasn't an easy conversation. There were questions, concerns, and moments when it felt like the outcome could go either way. But we stayed the course, emphasizing the shared mission between Morris Brown and the AME Church to uplift and educate the next generation of leaders.

By February 2020, the AME Church made a historic decision; they forgave the $3.5 million debt and accepted our scholarship proposal. It was a moment of relief, triumph, and gratitude all rolled into one. We had turned a monumental challenge into an opportunity to strengthen our bond with the AME Church and invest in the future of its students.

Since then, we have kept our promise, providing full tuition scholarships to eligible AME students and meeting our obligations under the agreement. This wasn't just a financial victory; it was a testament to our strategic thinking and steady focus on the goal of reaccreditation.

That moment marked a turning point, a reminder that with determination, collaboration, and faith, even the most insurmountable obstacles can be overcome. It was one more step forward in the long journey to rebuild Morris Brown College.

Stepping into the role of CFO at Morris Brown College during one of its most turbulent times was both humbling and overwhelming. This wasn't just a professional challenge—it was deeply personal. Morris Brown wasn't just another institution; it was my alma mater, a place steeped in history and rich with legacy. To be one of the people entrusted with its survival was an honor I couldn't take lightly.

But let's be honest—it was a monumental task. Morris Brown had been operating as an unaccredited HBCU since 2002, and the weight of that reality was impossible to ignore. The stakes were high, and the to-do list seemed endless. On one end, I was tasked with cleaning up six years' worth of financial statements—a mountain of numbers, transactions, and unanswered questions that spanned nearly a decade. On the other hand, I still had the daily accounting responsibilities that kept the college running. Balancing both was no small feat.

Every day brought something new, often in the form of a surprise I hadn't anticipated. A missing file, a forgotten invoice, an error buried deep in the records. It felt like solving a puzzle with half the pieces missing. And yet, with every step forward, I was reminded of why I had taken on this role in the first place. This wasn't just about numbers or financial compliance. It was about preserving the soul of Morris Brown, ensuring that future generations could walk through its doors and find a place where they belonged.

The stress was real, but so was the determination. For me, this wasn't just a job; it was a mission. Morris Brown had given me so much, and now, it was my turn to give back.

There were moments when doubt whispered in my ear, and the fear of failure loomed like a shadow. The pressure was immense. The weight of knowing that the future of Morris Brown College—its students, its legacy, and the livelihoods of so many—rested on my shoulders was overwhelming. I couldn't shake the thought: *If I didn't succeed, the doors of Morris Brown could close forever—and it would happen on my watch.*

When I first stepped into my office, I was greeted not by order but by chaos—a visual representation of years of unresolved financial turmoil. Stacks of unopened envelopes towered precariously on the desk. Boxes of records were scattered across the floor and tucked away in storage areas, some so dusty that it was clear they hadn't been touched in years. The backlog of unaudited accounts stretched all the way back to 2015, a haunting reminder of just how much had been left undone.

It wasn't just the sheer volume of work that made the task feel insurmountable—it was the significance of every single piece of paper, every transaction, every unchecked line item. Each represented a part of the story we needed to tell: a story of survival, resilience, and financial stability. Every document had the potential to be the key that unlocked another door, or the answer to a question that had long gone unanswered.

I couldn't afford to let the fear paralyze me. Instead, I took it as a call to action. Slowly, methodically, I began sifting through the chaos, determined to bring order to the disorder and piece together the larger puzzle. Because failure wasn't just a personal fear—it was a risk Morris Brown simply couldn't afford.

Chapter 6

The scent of burnt carpet still lingered in the air, a sharp reminder of what had been lost—and what was at stake. The administration had spent months proving to the world that Morris Brown College was on the verge of a historic comeback. Yet, on the morning of February 11, 2020, flames licked at the edges of that dream.

The fire, deliberately set, had consumed the vice president of academic affairs' office, leaving behind scorched chairs, blackened walls, and an eerie silence. Investigators found a gas can near the broken window and fingerprints smudged against the glass. It wasn't a robbery. It wasn't an accident. It was a message.

Really? Two fires in one year? The only functional building we had left, targeted again. Was this a sign that Morris Brown wasn't meant to rise from the ashes? Was I insane to believe otherwise?

For a moment, I wavered. I had poured everything into this fight—sleepless nights, endless meetings, sacrificing the growth of my CPA firm to help revive my alma mater. I turned to my sisters, to my inner circle of pastors and prayer warriors, searching for clarity. And then, as if whispered in the quiet, the answer came: Keep moving.

One month later, the next battle arrived, and the world was about to change, but none of us knew it yet.

***

The news hit like a distant rumble of thunder—subtle at first, then impossible to ignore. COVID-19 was no longer just a story on the evening news or a crisis unfolding overseas. It was here, in Georgia, creeping into daily conversations and filling inboxes with urgent messages from health officials.

An email from Dr. James landed in my inbox, carrying a tone that was firm but calm: "Your safety is my top priority. As you are aware, the coronavirus is spreading. There have been five cases confirmed in Georgia. While there is no need for panic, I ask that we all safeguard ourselves from the spread of germs."

The message went on, detailing safety measures—no handshakes, daily sanitization of doorknobs, a stockpile of Clorox wipes, and hand sanitizer stationed throughout the building. It was a checklist of precautions that, at the time, felt more like an inconvenience than a necessity. Still, something in my gut told me this was just the beginning.

The Georgia Department of Public Health was coordinating with the CDC, preparing for what they called a "potential outbreak." The email reassured us that the overall risk remained low, but the undercurrent of concern was undeniable. Officials spoke in measured tones, drawing comparisons to hurricane preparedness, but I knew this wasn't a storm we could see coming from miles away.

I read the list of recommended precautions: Wash your hands. Don't touch your face. Avoid close contact. Stay home if you're sick. Basic, almost elementary advice, yet the weight of it felt different now. The mention of possible school closures and canceled events sent a chill through me.

Morris Brown had already weathered so much—fires, financial struggles, the fight for accreditation. And now, this.

Was this just another challenge to overcome, another test of resilience? Or was it something far worse, a crisis that could shake the very foundation of everything we'd been working toward?

I closed my laptop and exhaled slowly. No one had the answers yet. But one thing was certain—life as we knew it was about to change.

During the pandemic, Latoya Washington, the lead external auditor of The Wesley Peachtree Group, CPAs, played a critical role in ensuring that our audited financial statements remained up-to-date. One night, as we worked tirelessly to complete Morris Brown's audit at 3:00 AM, she called me an hour later to discuss outstanding issues. As an essential worker, I made my way to the office from time to time, ensuring we stayed on track.

Keith Terrell, CPA, and our supervisor, provided encouragement and guidance. His support was invaluable, helping us navigate these challenges. The Wesley Peachtree Group, a Black-owned CPA firm in Atlanta, Georgia, prides itself on fostering a collaborative and supportive environment, and Keith's leadership exemplified this. In the end, everyone's hard work paid off.

After eighteen months under this new Administration, we were finally ready to apply for reaccreditation candidacy with TRACS. By this point, we had incurred over $80,000 in expenses, including required audits, consulting and legal fees. However, donations from alumni and other stakeholders continued to flow in, fueling our efforts.

On November 11, 2020—amid the COVID-19 pandemic— President James sent an internal memo to faculty and staff announcing that our TRACS application had been approved. That same day, the Atlanta Business Chronicle published an article highlighting this historic milestone. Then, on January 5, 2021, he informed stakeholders that TRACS would be conducting a site visit that day, with the goal of achieving candidacy by April 2021. Internally, he outlined our plan to reapply for federal financial aid, which we had lost in 2003, emphasizing that the bankruptcy would not hinder the application. We immediately began working with the U.S. Department of Education to confirm and proceed with the process.

Administratively, extensive preparations for the TRACS visit had already been implemented. The Registrar's office updated course codes in the student catalog. Financial Aid developed Title IV policies and procedures while finalizing the application for submission to the Department of Education. The Student Accounts Department ensured that students with outstanding balances were on payment plans. Academic Affairs, led by then-Provost Dr. Anthony Johnson, refined academic policies to support student success. Institutional Advancement documented donations and pledges to secure long-term financial stability. Human Resources verified that department chairpersons and instructors met qualification requirements. The Facilities team painted, completed minor building improvements, and ensured code compliance. Additionally, a hospitality team was formed to coordinate accommodation for the TRACS evaluation team.

Amid these preparations, Morris Brown faced an unexpected setback—Fountain Hall, a historic landmark, was vandalized in December 2020. Spray paint defaced paintings, and windows were shattered. Fortunately, the Morris Brown College Focus Group donated $15,000 specifically for the building's restoration. We allocated a portion of these funds to secure the site and begin preparations for installing security cameras. Despite this unfortunate incident, our momentum remained strong as we approached the long-awaited TRACS visit.

The week of January 5, 2021, arrived, and our team was ready. The TRACS team conducted a comprehensive review of our operations, and we anticipated the outcome: Morris Brown would be granted candidate status for reaccreditation.

Achieving "candidate for reaccreditation" status meant that the college had met the preliminary requirements set by TRACS, signifying significant progress toward full accreditation. This designation validated our commitment to maintaining and improving educational quality and institutional effectiveness.

During the visit, key faculty and staff were interviewed and, in some cases, asked to provide additional documentation to support the information in our application. My office was responsible for Institutional Eligibility Requirement #11 (IER #11).

In order for us to meet this requirement, we had to demonstrate that the college possessed sufficient financial strength to sustain its operations, student services, and academic programs. This included completing external financial audits within five months of the fiscal year's end to confirm financial stability, as well as maintaining access to credit lines or liquid reserves to ensure uninterrupted operations.

In TRACS' final report, they noted that Morris Brown had made substantial financial improvements. The $4.3 million debt forgiveness from the African Methodist Episcopal Church, successful fundraising initiatives, extensive promotion, historic landmark grants, Paycheck Protection Program (PPP) funding, and strategic partnerships all contributed to the institution's financial turnaround. External audit reports reflected a positive change in net assets over the past two years.

Finally, in a letter dated April 21, 2021, we received the official notification: the TRACS Accreditation Committee had voted to grant Morris Brown College candidate status for accreditation.

It was a historic day—a moment of triumph. We celebrated briefly, but the journey was far from over. I was mentally and physically exhausted, but we still had to finish the #HardReset. The next goal was clear: achieving full accreditation and restoration of financial aid within the next year.

Chapter 7

Morris Brown's loss of its accreditation in 2002 dealt a devastating blow, making the institution ineligible for federal financial aid. Without this crucial funding, student enrollment plummeted, and the college faced an existential crisis. Most prospective students, reliant on federal assistance, could no longer afford to attend, leading to a sharp decline in revenue.

After receiving the green light from TRACS that we were accredited, our financial aid director, Stephanie Gunby, with over twenty years of Title IV experience, made a huge discovery. While reviewing the Department of Education's Federal Student Aid Handbook, she found a provision stating that "a school is not eligible if it files for bankruptcy or has an order for bankruptcy." Our 2015 bankruptcy filing had lingering consequences, continuing to prevent Morris Brown from accessing Title IV federal financial aid. Without this support, tuition remained out of reach for many students. However, Morris Brown remained steadfast in its mission as a "Haven for all hungry souls."

Determined to challenge this policy, Dr. James and our general counsel leveraged personal connections with Department of Education officials to explore options for special consideration. Attorney Laurie Thomas, our general counsel at that time, played a pivotal role, drafting a compelling memo to the DOE arguing why Morris Brown should regain eligibility for Title IV funding. On April 14, 2021, her legal argument was presented to key decision-makers:

"Section 1002(4)(A) should not prevent the Department from approving Morris Brown to participate in the Title IV Programs because the statute is only intended to apply to institutions that declare bankruptcy while actively participating in the Title IV Programs, and therefore lose their eligibility as a result of declaring bankruptcy…"

At this stage, financial aid policy extended beyond my expertise. My background was in accounting and auditing, but Title IV regulations were unfamiliar territory. Unlike my firm's corporate clients, higher education had unique challenges, requiring me to rely on Attorney Thomas and her team to present a compelling case that Morris Brown's bankruptcy was firmly in the past. We weren't just seeking reinstatement—we were spearheading a historic HBCU revival.

During this uncertain period, morale among faculty and staff understandably wavered. Yet, their dedication to Morris Brown's mission never faltered. They worked diligently to support students and keep the institution running, their resilience serving as the foundation of our recovery.

As word of Morris Brown's fight for accreditation spread, other HBCUs took notice. Some institutions offered moral support and shared best practices, while others observed cautiously, waiting to see if our efforts would succeed before making public statements. Morris Brown's journey was more than an institutional comeback—it was a beacon of hope for other HBCUs facing similar struggles.

By the 2020–2021 academic year, we began to see signs of renewal. Our enrollment, which had shrunk to the brink of extinction, grew to forty-five students. That number may seem small on paper, but to us, it was monumental. It was proof that hope had returned to the campus. That our work wasn't in vain.

And while the public saw that number as progress, few could imagine the work happening behind the scenes to make that growth sustainable. While our general counsel fought to demonstrate that Morris Brown had the right to rejoin the Title IV federal student aid program, one of our unsung heroes—our financial aid director—was waging her own battle, largely alone.

With no staff and no margin for error, she took on the massive responsibility of creating the College's Title IV handbook from scratch. She coordinated financial aid training for our Provost, Department Chairs, and Accounting Department, and partnered with Dr. Gloria, our Provost, to prepare a painstaking fifty-eight-page application that detailed every program we wanted to qualify for federal student aid. These programs were required to lead to recognized credentials, prepare students for gainful employment, and meet the strict federal standards of instructional time and credit hours.

She didn't stop there. She requested approval for the full range of aid: Pell Grants, Perkins Loans, SEOG, and Work-Study, as well as Direct Subsidized and Unsubsidized Loans and PLUS Loans. She also established the compliance structure from the ground up—creating internal checks and balances, separating functions of awarding and disbursing aid, initiating regular reconciliation procedures, opening a dedicated Title IV bank account, drafting job descriptions for financial aid staff, and working with our registrar to assign proper CIP codes to academic programs.

She did all this quietly and without fanfare. Her work was the infrastructure we needed but couldn't see—an invisible scaffolding that held our dreams in place.

Finally, on March 4, 2022, we were informed of a significant development that was not anticipated twenty years ago. Dr. James sent an internal memo to key staff members indicating his expectation that Morris Brown College would be voted as a full member of the Transnational Association of Christian Colleges and Schools on April 22, 2022. He subsequently held a meeting with the team to acknowledge our efforts and dedication leading to this event. During the meeting in the conference room, my thoughts drifted to my initial days at Morris Brown College, including the process of obtaining financial aid.

I recalled graduating with Dr. Samuel Jolley as the president and Phylicia Rashad as the keynote speaker. My mind then shifted to an alumni meeting in 2002, where we were informed about the loss of our SACS accreditation. Students who had legacy connections still matriculated through this historical unaccredited HBCU. They went on to enter graduate school and have highly successful careers. *Our doors never closed*. Finally, I felt relieved. Todd appeared similarly affected by the news.

Unable to contain our emotions, Todd and I found ourselves overwhelmed, tears streaming down our faces. We both struggled to find the right words to express what we felt. The sense of achievement, relief, and deep connection to our shared experience was simply beyond description. Most of all, I was finally comfortable with openly acknowledging that I played a key role in Morris Brown's restoration. I served as the Chief Financial Officer during this critical period in the school's history. I led the charge to re-create responsible financial management. The small team that I led contributed to efforts to improve the college's financial stability, including managing audits and ensuring financial compliance. The financial statements told the story of the impact of a $4 million debt forgiveness on the college's accreditation process. My work as CFO was integral to the college's ability to meet the financial requirements for accreditation. I cemented my legacy in the restoration of my alma mater, Morris Brown College. Within days (or even hours) of Dr. James's announcement, the word had spread like wildfire. Morris Brown did what seemed impossible. We regained our accreditation after nearly twenty years. I do not know of any HBCU that has ever achieved such an accomplishment. By April 22, 2022, when TRACS made its formal announcement, the jubilation had already started. At the press conference held that day, hundreds of current students, alumni, local politicians, and community leaders attended. News crews were there as well. I believe I cried throughout the entire event as I felt the stress of getting to this point fall off my shoulders. A local news reporter walked over to me after the event to inquire about my emotions. She noticed me during the press conference. I explained that as an alumnus and current CFO, this was surreal and I was so elated to have had a role in Morris Brown's historic comeback.

One month later, on May 19, 2022, Alpha Kappa Alpha Sorority, Incorporated® surprised us with another gift. Our former International President and CEO, Dr. Glenda Glover and President of Tennessee State University (her alma mater), traveled to our campus to personally deliver a check for $100,000 to establish an endowment for scholarships and provide for other operating costs. It was part of our HBCU for Life: A Call to Action initiative. We were flanked by Dr. James, alumni and current students, along with dozens of members of our Sorority, including the ladies of Gamma Gamma chapter.

Chapter 8

Morris Brown College was never just a college to me. It was the place where I first discovered my worth. It's where I stood in cap and gown, degree in hand, and felt for the first time that I was walking into my purpose. So, when the call came in 2019 asking me to return—not as a student, but as a leader—I didn't walk into that role as CFO just for a paycheck. I walked in on faith, believing in the mission and the miracle.

Faith would have to carry me, because the challenges were like nothing I had ever faced. A small fire damaged part of our building. A flood soaked our floors. Financial audits tested our systems, and bureaucratic red tape slowed every step of our progress.

When my colleague Todd, a former classmate of my older sister, fell ill during the summer of 2023, I stepped in to assume his duties. I helped plan the Homecoming Saturday festivities on the yard, unaware that I, too, was facing a serious health issue. In December of the same year, almost two months after Todd returned to work, I suffered a stroke and was out of the office for a month. During that time, the controller managed the day-to-day operations, including bill payments, student accounts, and all fiscal affairs functions in between.

And still, I showed up even when fear of another stroke loomed, and the overwhelming responsibility of managing everything without an accounting staff weighed heavily on me. I kept going because I saw myself in those students, the ones who dared to enroll at a school with no accreditation, no dorms, and no guarantees. Students who were betting on possibility. Who, like me, had learned early on that Black dreams require not just hard work, but extraordinary faith.

And through it all, I learned this: legacy isn't what you leave behind. It's what you build while you're still here. Sometimes it looks like writing policies late at night, answering emails from a cell phone in a hospital bed, or standing in boardrooms where no one expects you to speak with authority—until you do.

Coming full circle didn't feel like a celebration. It felt like a fight. But it was worth it.

Looking back now, I realize that coming back to Morris Brown wasn't just about saving a college. It was about healing a piece of myself. The young woman who once crossed that campus full of ambition had returned—older, wiser, tested—and determined to stand in the gap for the next generation.

Legacy doesn't always look like a statue or a plaque on the wall. Sometimes it looks like unpaid weekends, prayers over spreadsheets, and one determined woman writing a fifty-eight-page application that could change the course of a college's future.

Indeed, we not only managed to endure but also excelled in every aspect.

Morris Brown is no longer a story of what was lost. It's a story of what was reclaimed through resilience, through grace, through relentless belief.

So, if you take nothing else from my story, let it be this: When God calls you back, go, even if it costs you. Even if you're afraid. Even if you don't know where the road leads. Because obedience will always lead you home.

Looking to the Future

Chapter 9

The journey of Morris Brown College wasn't just about reclaiming accreditation—it was about reclaiming our legacy, our purpose, and our hope. Standing today on the same grounds that were once nearly abandoned, I now see students strolling along the pathways, heading to renovated classrooms, and gathering in spaces that echo with laughter, ambition, and promise. The air is electric, filled with the powerful energy of dreams reborn.

In the wake of our reaccreditation, enrollment surged. From just a handful of students, we grew steadily, first dozens, then hundreds. Each new student who walks onto our campus represents a new chapter in the ongoing story of Morris Brown. They arrive hopeful, ready to contribute to our community and carry forward the legacy we fought so hard to restore.

Our programs, too, have blossomed. With renewed support, we launched partnerships with local businesses, strengthened internship opportunities, and expanded scholarship offerings, especially for those committed to the AME Church students. We established innovative academic pathways, emphasizing technology, entrepreneurship, and social justice—areas critical for empowering the next generation of Black leaders. The campus hums with vitality, innovation, and vision, a testament to what can happen when people unite behind a common cause.

Morris Brown's journey is more than just a triumph of institutional renewal. It is proof of what collective resilience, unwavering faith, and shared purpose can achieve. Our story has inspired other HBCUs nationwide, providing a blueprint for institutions facing similar struggles. We are no longer a cautionary tale; we are a beacon of hope.

I reflect often on those early mornings and late nights in my cluttered office, the stacks of unopened envelopes, the overwhelming feeling of uncertainty, and the quiet prayers whispered in moments of exhaustion. Those days tested my faith, but they also deepened it. Through the fires, through illness, through doubt, and through triumph, I learned a powerful lesson: legacy is not what you leave behind—it's what you build each day through your actions, your choices, and your sacrifices.

As I stand now, gazing out of my office window toward Fountain Hall, I see clearly how deeply intertwined my journey is with the place I call home. Morris Brown didn't just shape me—it summoned me back, gave me purpose, and helped me discover strengths within myself I never knew existed.

Students pass by, aware of the battles, but struggle to understand how hard we fought to keep these grounds alive. They laugh, dream, and walk confidently toward their futures, just as generations before them once did. Watching them, I feel immense pride and deep fulfillment. Our past struggles made their bright futures possible.

In the silence of this moment, my heart swells with gratitude. Gratitude for the courage to say yes to a call I almost didn't answer. Gratitude for the community that never stopped believing. And gratitude to God, whose guiding hand carried me through it all.

This isn't just Morris Brown's rebirth. It's my rebirth, too. And from this sacred space, filled with the echoes of history and hope, I look ahead with confidence, knowing our best days are not behind us—they are just beginning. I am so thankful that Morris Brown College prepared me to walk into my calling and eventually save the Institution I hold dearly in my heart.

Morris Brown College
Alma Mater

Chapter 10

Alma Mater,

pride of earth,

Gav'st to me another birth,

Haven for all hungry souls,

Feeding them shall be Thy goal,

Ever let thy banner be,

Emblem of the brave and free,

A welcome true to everyone,

Until Thy work is done.

Hail to Thee, maker of men,

Honor to Thee once again,

Sacred truths on firmest ground,

Hail to Thee, Dear Morris Brown.

To her precepts praise accord,

To them may we e'er be bound,

And bow and thank the gracious Lord,

dear ol' Morris Brown.

Lyrics: Milton Randolph

Music: E. Waymon Hathcock